Northbrook Public Library
3 1123 01117 9622

W9-BYL-834

HARLEY-DAVIDSON

The story of a motoring icon

Mason Crest

Contents

Mason Crest
450 Parkway Drive, Suite D
Broomall, PA 19008
www.masoncrest.com

Printed and bound in the United States of America.

10 9 8 7 6 5 4 3 2 1

Cataloging-in-Publication Data on file with the Library of Congress.

Series ISBN: 978-1-4222-3275-0
Hardback ISBN: 978-1-4222-3280-4
ebook ISBN: 978-1-4222-8518-3

Written by: Clyde Hawkins

Images courtesy of PA Photos, Mary Evans Picture Library and Wiki Commons

Introduction

As so often happens in success stories, one person may have the spark of an idea but it is not until all the components come together that a legend is born. In the case of Harley-Davidson motorcycles, it was William Harley who first drew up plans for an engine to be fitted to a bicycle frame, but it was not until he teamed up with Arthur Davidson and his brothers that their embryonic mode of transport became a reality that has endured – although not necessarily always thrived – for more than a century.

It is perhaps difficult for us to comprehend in the 21st century, with more than a billion examples in worldwide use, but the first bicycle (derived from "bi" meaning "two" and "cycle" coming from the Latin "cyclus," originating from the Greek "kyklos" meaning "circle, wheel, any circular body, circular motion, cycle of events") was only created in 1817. German inventor Baron Karl Drais presented his Laufmaschine ("running machine") – a frame set on two wheels but rather than being powered by pedals it was propelled along by the rider pushing their feet on the ground (rather like the balance bikes used today to teach children how to balance and steer without them having to concentrate on pedaling as well).

It is unclear exactly when the first mechanically-driven bicycle was built but most credit

■ ABOVE: The Laufmaschine (running machine). It is displayed at the Kurpfälzisches Museum in Heidelberg, Germany.

■ OPPOSITE: Motorcyclists parade through the streets of Mexico City, commemorating the 110th anniversary of the Harley-Davidson; according to organizers an estimated 5,000 riders participated, 2013.

P. LALLEMENT.
VELOCIPEDE.

No. 59,915. Patented Nov. 20, 1866.

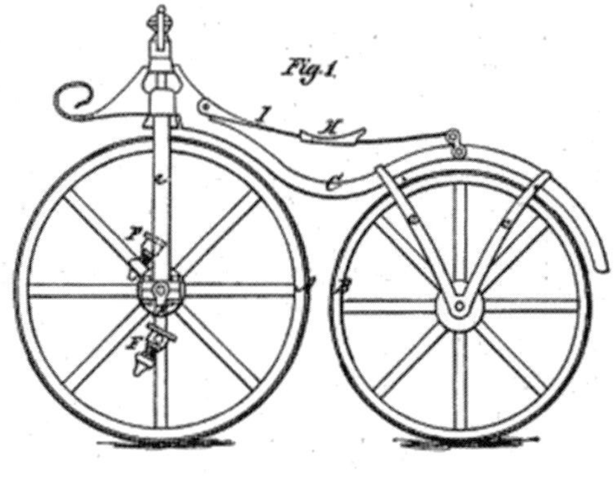

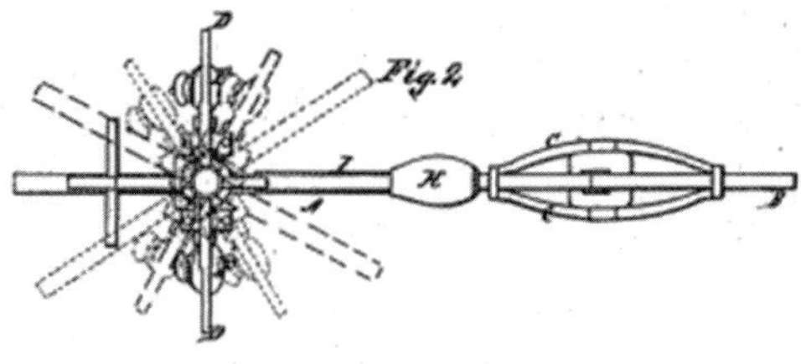

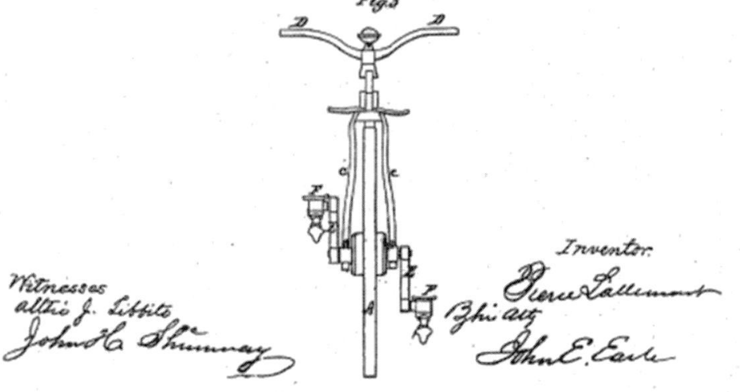

Frenchmen Pierre Michaux and Pierre Lallement, who added a mechanical crank drive with pedals on an enlarged front wheel (the velocipede) in the early 1860s. Following this innovation, it was only a matter of time before another genius discovered a way of making it less strenuous for the rider… It was Michaux & Co who paved the way, with their steam velocipede in 1867, when Ernest Michaux (Pierre's son) added a small steam engine to power the vehicle. Lallement, meanwhile, claimed he had come up with the idea in 1863 and filed for the US patent in 1866.

Numerous inventors tried their hand at perfecting the steam-powered bicycle (a term that replaced velocipede from about 1868 onward), with two producing machines in 1868. American Sylvester H. Roper's innovation was to install a coal-fired boiler to power his twin-cylinder steam engine, while Frenchman Louis-Guillaume Perreaux's offering was a single-cylinder engine fitted to a Michaux frame fueled by an alcohol burner under the saddle, which he patented the following year.

The major change in the 19th-

■ **ABOVE: The patent for the velocipede dated 1866.**

■ **RIGHT: The steam velocipede at The Art of the Motorcycle exhibition, New York, 1999.**

century motorcycle industry was kickstarted by the widespread commercial drilling and refining of oil in the 1850s. While oil has been extracted from the ground since the 4th century in China, the first commercial oil well was in Oil Springs, Ontario, and entered production in 1858. There had already been numerous attempts to create an internal combustion engine, small yet powerful enough to propel vehicles, but it was German inventor Gottlieb Daimler who is credited with creating the first internal combustion-engined motorcycle (the Reitwagen) with his business partner Wilhelm Maybach, in 1885. The same year, fellow German engineer Karl Benz (who had patented his first engine in 1879) unveiled the first gasoline-powered automobile – the Motorwagen. Horse power would soon have a completely different meaning!

The United States, however, lagged behind Europe in its fascination with two-wheeled speed, and legend has it that the first motorcycle only arrived in the country as late as 1895 when a French circus act turned up to perform in New York. The same year, though, American inventor E.J. Pennington showed off his first bike – allegedly capable of 58 mph (93 kmh) – in Milwaukee and reportedly coined the term "motorcycle."

It wasn't long before a host of manufacturers (such as Indian, Excelsior, and Merkel) sprang up, and they were quickly developing and improving this new technology. So, while the motorcycle was still in its infancy when Harley began his journey and teamed up with the Davidsons, the road to fame and success was there for the taking.

■ ABOVE: The Reitwagen was invented by Gottleib Daimler.

Origins and Early Years

For such an American institution to be able to trace its roots to the United Kingdom is perhaps a surprise to many, but that is exactly where the Harley-Davidson heritage begins. The Davidsons emigrated to the US from Aberdeen in Scotland in the second half of the 19th century, while the Harleys made a similar journey but from Manchester in the north of England. Both decided to settle in Milwaukee, Wisconsin, to start families of their own.

William Harley (born on December 29, 1880) and Arthur Davidson (February 11, 1881) were childhood friends with a shared passion for cycling and fishing. It has been mooted that their foray into the world of engine design could have been instigated by wishing to improve their enjoyment of either pastime, so when Harley came up with the idea for a small engine in 1901 it was only natural that he turned to Davidson to bring his dream to fruition. Bill worked as a draughtsman for the local Barth Manufacturing Company, who also employed Arthur as a pattern maker. Arthur also had two older brothers – William, a foreman on the Milwaukee railways, and Walter, a machinist in Kansas – so the four men who would lay the foundations for Harley-Davidson had the perfect engineering backgrounds.

Bill and Arthur worked on developing the engine in a wooden shed erected in the garden of the Davidson family home with workmates Emile Kruger and Ole Evinrude, who sorted them out with a carburetor. Even Walter, who moved back to the area in 1902, became fascinated with the venture and got involved. When the 10 cubic inch (164 cubic centimeter) engine was ready, they installed it in a bicycle frame, but their first effort was not powerful enough to cope with the hills around their hometown so they set about creating an improved version. This boasted a more powerful 25 ci (410 cc) engine that was comfortable doing 25 mph (40 kmh) but now the trouble was that the frame was vibrating, cracking, and obviously not up to the job. The only solution was to fabricate a more suitable, sturdier frame that could cope with the stresses, and so the first Harley-Davidson motorcycle was born although, in reality, it still resembled a bicycle with pedals and a lack of gears or suspension.

This early machine soon established a reputation for reliability and, as orders started to be received, the Harley-Davidson Motor Company was born in 1903. While Bill took himself off to the University of Wisconsin to study an engineering degree, Arthur built two customer-ordered bikes – one for school friend Henry Meyer – that winter as their hobby seemed to be becoming more of a vocation. This became an eventuality as production increased and the first Harley-Davidson dealer – C.H. Lang in Chicago – opened in 1904. Carl Herman Lang sold three of the first five production bikes. The way in which the pistons connect to the crank produce a sound that

■ ABOVE: Founders of the Harley-Davidson Motor Co.: William A. Davidson, vice president and works manager; Walter Davidson, president and general manager; Arthur Davidson, secretary and sales manager; William S. Harley, treasurer and chief engineer.

■ OPPOSITE: Serial Number One, the very first Harley-Davidson motorcycle, displayed at the Harley-Davidson Museum in Milwaukee.

is unique to Harley-Davidsons and owners have cherished that "rumble" from the outset.

On July 4, 1905, Harley-Davidson entered and won a 15-mile race in Chicago and Walter left his day job the same year to work full-time for the firm. Harley-Davidson moved to a purpose-built factory on Chestnut Street (later Juneau Avenue) in 1906, where 49 bikes (nicknamed Silent Gray Fellows after their paintwork) were produced in the first year. The fledgling company now boasted six employees and registered a world first with the publication of a motorcycle catalog. By the time Bill had graduated in 1907, 152 Harley-Davidsons were being manufactured a year and the company was incorporated, with Harley and the three Davidson brothers as stockholders. Arthur was being kept busy demonstrating the bike to potential dealers – specifically targeting New England – while William was brought in as factory manager.

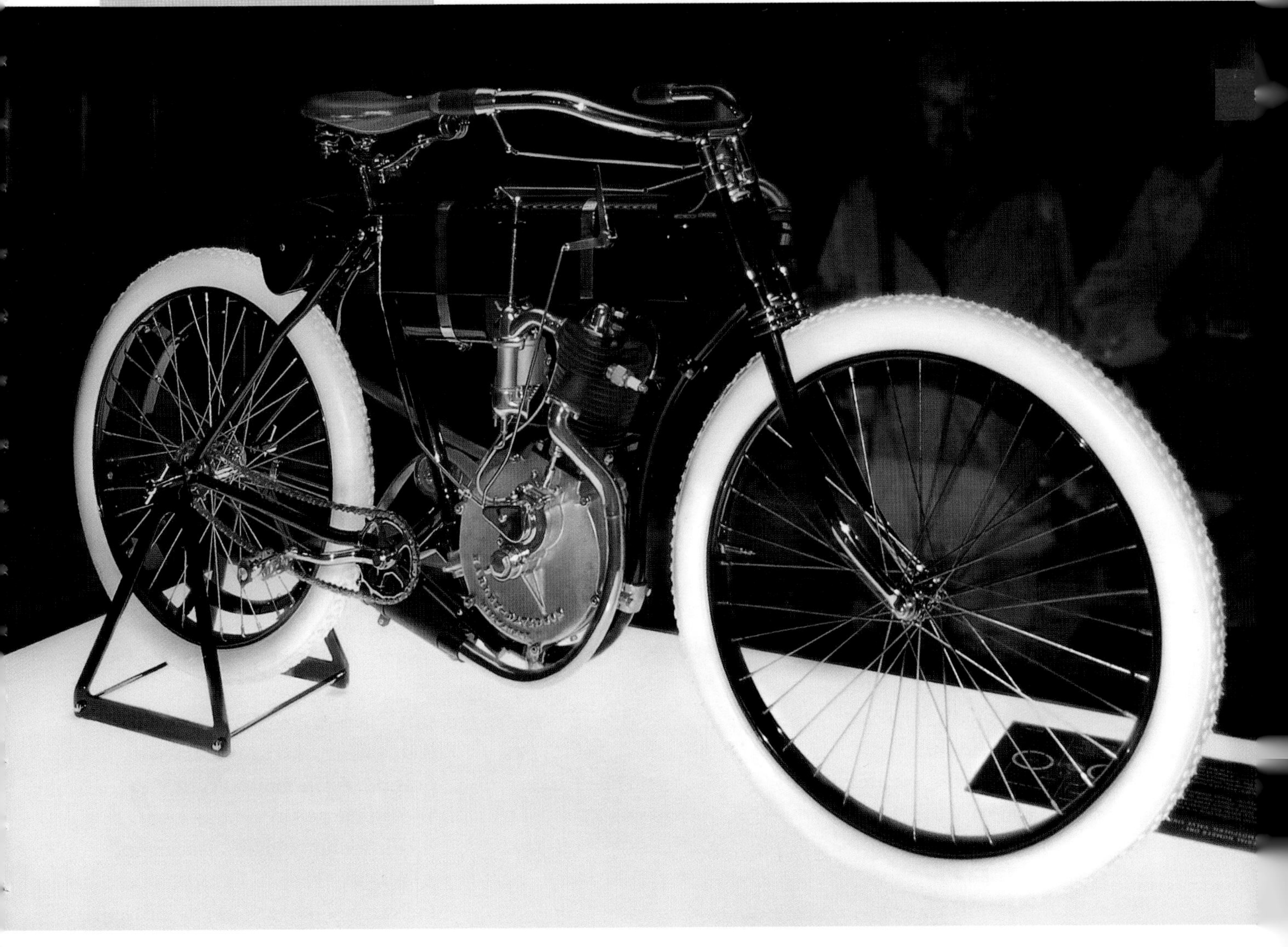

Walter entered the 7th Annual Federation of American Motorcyclists' (FAM) Endurance and Reliability Contest in 1908 and scored a perfect 1,000 points. Three days later, he set a new FAM economy record of 188.234 miles per gallon and the number of bikes manufactured again trebled as the business grew. The company also began supplying motorcycles to the Detroit Police Department. But as the business expanded, so did the number of riders and the distances traveled and they began to

demand more powerful machines, which led to the introduction of the company's first V-twin. The engine size of the single had increased to 30 ci (494 cc) in 1909, but Bill Harley had greater ambitions and paired two singles onto a crankcase at a 45-degree angle to create a 49 ci (803 cc) twin the same year. In theory this should have doubled the power output but, unfortunately, the twin was no faster than the single and caused the drive belt to slip so was dropped and redesigned for its 1911 reappearance.

■ ABOVE: **Walter Davidson with his Harley-Davidson motorcycle, 1908.**

By this time, the inlet valves had been modified to be mechanically operated by pushrods, as opposed to the previously atmospheric system that relied on engine vacuum, and four-figure engine revs were possible. A tensioning device was also introduced to minimize any power loss through the drivetrain. This F-Head engine – named after the shape of the valve ports – proved

■ **ABOVE:** **A Harley-Davidson motorcycle advertisement for the Silent Gray Fellow in 1915.**

so successful for Harley-Davidson that it remained in production until the end of the 1920s, although a 61 ci (1,000 cc) variant was introduced in 1912 that could produce 11 hp.

One icon that appeared in 1910, and has been a staple of Harley-Davidson ever since, was the now instantly recognizable bar and shield logo. The same year saw competitive racing success across the United States with seven H-D riders winning events such as

hillclimbs and endurance contests. This continued and the Racing Department, headed by Bill Harley with William Ottaway as assistant engineer, was formed two years later.

By the time the factory was enlarged to a six-story building in 1912, the production of Harley-Davidsons had surpassed an annual total of 5,600 bikes. The company now offered parts and accessories and could boast more than 200 dealers nationwide. They also began exporting H-Ds to Japan, and by the end of the following year were manufacturing around 13,000 machines.

The single was upgraded in 1913, with engine capacity growing to 35 ci (565 cc) and the adoption of the mechanical inlet valves. Available in either belt- or chain-driven versions it was affectionately designated the 5-35 (based on figures of 5 hp, 35 ci) and production would run until 1918. The company also briefly offered the Forecar Delivery Van based on a V-twin, but a dramatic turn of events was just around the corner.

■ **ABOVE:** **Visitors looks at a 1913 Harley-Davidson 9-E, during the 40th Tokyo Motorcycle Show in Tokyo, 2013.**

■ **LEFT:** **An army officer sits astride a "Silent Gray" Harley-Davidson, *Illustrated London News*, February 1916.**

The World at War

While the United States initially declared its neutrality and did not enter the First World War until April 1917, the hostilities had broken out on July 28, 1914, and the impact would be felt on a global scale. But in peaceful America in 1914, Harley-Davidson was continuing to strive and perfect its motorcycles.

The introduction of clutch and brake pedals on both F-Head single and twin machines proved a welcome boon for riders, who could let the engine idle instead of starting the bike again every time they stopped. A two-speed rear hub was also briefly introduced; designed and patented by Bill Harley, it was soon superseded the following year by a three-speed that improved the drivetrain function. One of the fundamental flaws in the drivetrain at the time, however, was the belt drive: leather belts were prone to rot, stretch, and therefore slip but Harley-Davidson would be

■ LEFT: A Lambert & Butler cigarette card featuring a Harley-Davidson with sidecar, 1923.

■ OPPOSITE: A First World War advertisement for the Harley-Davidson Motor Company, showing an officer riding a motorcycle and gallantly helping a fashionably dressed lady into its sidecar.

■ BELOW: An Italian advertisement for a Harley-Davidson with sidecar, 1921.

■ **ABOVE: Leslie Parkhurst sits astride the Harley-Davidson that took him to a new motorcycle world land speed record at Daytona Beach, Florida.**

one of the last major manufacturers to change over completely to the more efficient chain design. The company offered models with sidecars from 1914 as well and these proved popular in an era when even the cheapest automobile was too expensive for the average person.

Sidecar design was another technology that was in its infancy but it gave a more comfortable option for transporting a passenger than perching on the pillion seat. One innovator was Hugo H. Young, a graphic designer who had opened a Harley-Davidson agency in 1910, and he recognized that a flexible connection between the motorcycle and sidecar was a preferred option. His first design appeared in 1912; by 1916 it had been modified to allow the sidecar wheel to remain on the ground to provide greater stability even when the bike was leaning going around corners. The Flxible Sidecar Company was incorporated in 1914 and began supplying Harley-Davidson as well as other motorcycle manufacturers. As automobiles became more affordable in the 1920s, however, sidecars became a less common sight on the highways, and the United States' ban on sidecar racing in 1925, following numerous fatal accidents, diminished their popularity even more.

With the H-D Racing Department having been in existence for two years, they officially joined the motorcycle racing circuit in 1914. It wouldn't take long for them to acquire the "Wrecking Crew" nickname in recognition of their dominance over their rivals, with legendary racers such as Leslie "Red" Parkhurst and Joe Petrali. Success in competitive racing was vital to boosting the public awareness and perception of a motorcycle brand and there was no one better at that than Harley-Davidson. They pulled ahead of their main competitor, Indian, and saw off many of the plethora of manufacturers that had sprung up in the first decade of the new century.

Another method of promoting a brand is through print, and

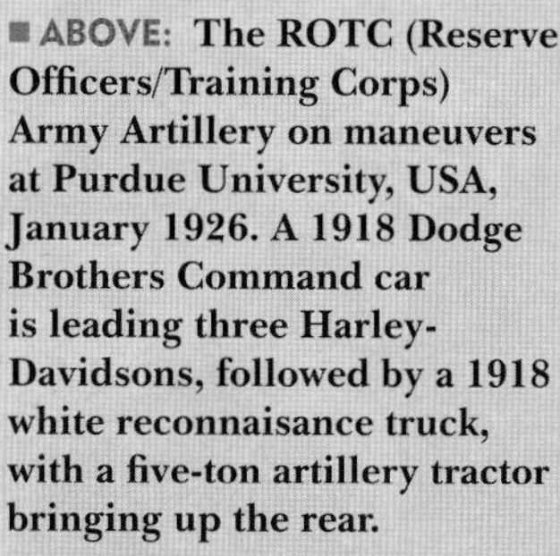

■ **ABOVE: The ROTC (Reserve Officers/Training Corps) Army Artillery on maneuvers at Purdue University, USA, January 1926. A 1918 Dodge Brothers Command car is leading three Harley-Davidsons, followed by a 1918 white reconnaisance truck, with a five-ton artillery tractor bringing up the rear.**

■ **OPPOSITE: Left to right: Bill Minick, Eddie Brink, and Joe Petrali who was a racer with the H-D Racing Department.**

■ **ABOVE: British racecar driver Sir Malcolm Campbell rides a Harley-Davidson before testing his Bluebird to a land speed record on the flat sands of Daytona Beach, Florida, 1935.**

Harley-Davidson launched *The Enthusiast* magazine in 1916, which has gone on to become the longest continually published title of the genre. Publication was sporadic initially but it became quarterly and was priced at 5c. Today, it is only available to members of the Harley Owners Group (HOG). The "Hog" nickname was first used in 1920 when victorious members of the H-D racing team carried a pig mascot with them on each victory lap.

As previously mentioned, the United States joined the war against Germany in April 1917, so it is no surprise that around 33 per cent of all Harley-Davidsons manufactured that year were sold to the military. The company also set up its Quartermasters' School to train army mechanics, and this would continue in civilian life as the Service School to provide dealers – who are now selling H-D motorcycles – with personnel specifically trained to maintain Harley-Davidsons. The following year, the final of the conflict, saw almost half of the production bikes sold to the US Army, and one in particular made headline news for the company. After the Armistice had been signed on November 11, 1918, Corporal Roy Holtz from

Wisconsin was the first American to enter Germany the following day and he was photographed doing so on a Harley-Davidson… As the decade ended, the 37 ci (606 cc) Sport model was introduced. With a horizontally (fore and aft) opposed twin engine, the Sport was extremely quiet and very popular.

Such was the meteoric rise of Harley-Davidson that they were the biggest motorcycle manufacturer in the world by the start of the 1920s, with some 2,000 dealers in 67 countries across the world. They built more than 18,000 bikes in 1920, compared to Indian's almost 20,000 – two years later and their competitor's output had fallen by two-thirds, while H-Ds were down one-third. This was largely due to Henry Ford, among others, and his affordable Model-T that would go on to sell more than 16 million by the time it ceased production in 1927…

The 1920s saw the introduction of the JD and FD models (1922) that boasted a 74 ci (1,200 cc) V-twin engine, the adoption of the teardrop gas tank (1925), and the reappearance of single cylinder bikes (1926). All Harley-Davidson models from 1928 were fitted with a front brake, which would be useful as the company's first twin cam engine was fitted to the JD series enabling the motorcycle to reach speeds up to 100 mph (160 kmh). The following year saw the arrival of the 45 ci (750 cc) V-twin engine on the D model. It would prove so reliable and popular – nicknamed the "flathead" – that it would be continually used in various guises until the 1970s. The year of 1929

■ BELOW: **Henry Ford, the American motor manufacturer, with his son Edsel, in one of the many versions of the Model-T.**

■ **ABOVE: A selection of Harley-Davidson gas tanks.**

is more globally remembered, however, for the stock market crash, leading to the Great Depression.

The company had sold more than 20,000 motorcycles in 1929... by 1933 this was down to 4,000 and there were only two American manufacturers left in existence – Harley-Davidson and Indian. The three-wheeled Servi-Car was unveiled in 1932 and became a common sight on the streets as police and commercial vehicles until the 1970s, while the following year saw the introduction of graphics on gas tanks in an effort to stimulate sales.

By 1935, high exchange rates were making it expensive for Harley-Davidson to export their bikes to Japan so the company's agent in Asia (Alfred Child) persuaded the company to license production to the Sankyo Seiyakyo Corporation. These Japanese-produced H-Ds were sold under the moniker Rikuo, which translates as "King of the Road."

The following year brought a new model – the 61 ci (1,000 cc) EL with its overhead valve (OHV) V-twin engine that was soon nicknamed the "knucklehead" due to its rocker-boxes – and a new engine in the 80 ci (1,300 cc) V-twin with side valves. A new land speed record was set in 1937, when Petrali reached 136.183 mph on a streamlined Knucklehead. That same year, the WL model was first produced and William Davidson – one of the founding fathers of the company – died.

While the 1930s had proved

difficult times for Harley-Davidson, the world had again gone to war on September 1, 1939, although the United States did not enter the affray until provoked by the Japanese attack on Pearl Harbor in December 1940. Production of motorcycles for civilian use was virtually non-existent during the Second World War, with the company manufacturing around 90,000 units for military use by the end of the conflict. The US Army did ask Harley-Davidson (and Indian) to come up with a model that was sturdier and better adapted to military life – the XA was born that shared many features with the BMW R71. Only around 1,000 of these shaft-driven 45 ci (750 cc) machines were manufactured; the Jeep was a more popular and versatile alternative and the XA never went into civilian production.

■ **ABOVE: A Rikuo RQ (1955) motorcycle.**

■ **BELOW: A Harley-Davidson XA military motorcycle.**

The Second World War may have been over, but millions had died during the six-year conflict and their loss was felt all around the world. At Harley-Davidson, two key members of staff – Walter Davidson (1942) and William Harley (1943) – were mourned as well, but the H-D journey stretched on into the distance.

A Return to Civilian Life

Harley-Davidson wasted no time in resuming production of civilian motorcycles, with output beginning in November 1945. As part of Germany's war reparations, the Allies helped themselves to ideas that German firms had patented that included the two-stroke engine developed by DKW for their popular RT125 motorcycle. Harley-Davidson adapted this for their Model S – launched in 1947 as a 1948 model – as did the British manufacturer BSA (with the Bantam) and the Soviet Union's MMZ (M1A Moskva, also known as the Minsk).

The Harley-Davidson 125 engine produced 3 hp and proved a successful route into motorcycling for many youngsters who would then work their way up to bigger machines. Although ignored by many dealers, more than 10,000 were sold during the first year of production. These lightweight

■ **ABOVE: A 1947 FL Harley-Davidson.**

H-Ds would continue to be manufactured in numerous forms until 1966 and have all since become affectionately known as Hummers. The Hummer was a 1955 model that was named after Dean Hummer, an Omaha-based dealer who championed the two-stroke.

Those who attended the 1947 Dealers' Convention were given a preview of the new factory on Capitol Drive that had been purchased to provide the facility to manufacture the components that were then sent to Juneau Avenue for assembly. The following year, the 61 ci (1,000 cc) and 74 ci (1,200 cc) OHV engines were revamped to include hydraulic valve lifters and aluminum heads that were topped with chrome-plated rocker covers. As these reminded people of baking pans it is only natural that they became known as "panheads." Another major improvement was the arrival of hydraulic forks in 1949, which made their first appearance on the recently launched Hydra Glide models.

The final surviving founding member of the company, Arthur Davidson, was killed in a car crash in 1950. The 69-year-old died along with his wife Clara and children Dorothy and Donald Jeffery when their vehicle hit another near their Waukesha home in Wisconsin.

The year of 1953 proved to be a memorable one as Harley-Davidson celebrated its half-century. A celebratory logo was designed that incorporated the H-D bar over a "V" – which symbolized the engine that had brought so much success to the company – with the words "50 years" above and "American made" below. It was perhaps ironic that their only remaining competitor (Indian) went out of business the same year, leaving Harley-Davidson as the only US motorcycle manufacturer.

For many servicemen, their first experience of riding a Harley-Davidson had been during the Second World War and there had been lots of converts, but some returning to the United States had grown fond of the lighter twin bikes they had encountered in the United Kingdom. In an attempt to appease these potential buyers, Harley-Davidson had launched the 45 ci (750 cc) K model in 1952 with a single-cast crankcase and transmission to minimize weight. These K models were the forerunner of the Sportster that was launched in 1957 and has been in production ever since. Featuring a 55 ci (900 cc) OHV engine, the Sportster soon became a much-loved member of the H-D family and was the first motorcycle to earn the "superbike" tag.

While 1958 had seen the introduction of hydraulic rear suspension on the Duo Glide, one of the most dramatic changes of direction came two years later. The company, recognizing the demand for smaller bikes, created the Topper and bought a 50 per cent stake in Aeronautica-Macchi (Aermacchi), an Italian outfit that had a reputation for exciting single-cylinder machines up to 21 ci (350 cc). The Topper was the only scooter Harley-Davidson has ever manufactured, with production running until 1965, and was powered by a 10 ci (165 cc) single-cylinder two-stroke engine that could reach 46 mph (74 kmh). Initial reaction was good, with almost 4,000 units being made in the first year, but this had dropped to just 500 by the end of the production run. The first fruit of the collaboration with Aermacchi was unveiled in 1961 with the Sprint, a 15 ci (250 cc) lightweight motorcycle that could hit a top speed of 70 mph (115

■ **ABOVE: The rear of a 1955 FLH Harley-Davidson.**

kmh). Further machines included the M-50 and M-60 as well as the SX-350 and SS-350 by the end of the 1970s.

As fiberglass usage became more widespread, Harley-Davidson invested in the Tomahawk Boat Manufacturing Company in 1962 and began experimenting with incorporating the lightweight material into their motorcycles. Further innovation arrived in 1964 when the Servi-Car received an electric starter (the Duo Glide was the next recipient the following year – being renamed the Electra Glide – with the new technology soon being rolled out across the range), while the "panhead" was replaced by the "shovelhead" in 1966. This new engine was more powerful but still weighed in at 74 ci (1,200 cc) and was enlarged to 82 ci (1,340 cc) in 1978 for the big V-twins.

■ ABOVE: **Japanese invasion competitor: a 1974 Honda CB750 K4 in sunrise orange.**

■ OPPOSITE: **John Gibson poses with his crew and his Harley-Davidson after winning the 200-mile American Motorcycle Association race, Daytona Beach, 1956.**

The 1960s ended with what turned out to be a disastrous sale to the American Machine and Foundry Company (AMF) as the invasion of Japanese competitors, such as the Honda CB750, was about to be unleashed. The AMF years are ones that most Harley-Davidson aficionados would happily forget as the build quality hit rock bottom. Dealer showrooms were littered with unsold bikes and their workshops full of ones that needed repairing under warranty. The number of motorcycles produced increased from a total of just over 16,000 in 1970 to a peak of over 47,000 just six years later.

Government legislation in the 1970s saw several changes being enforced with a return spring added to the throttle and the US DOT mandating a left-side shift for all new motorcycles, probably

■ **ABOVE: A 1971 FX Super Glide.**

■ **LEFT: A fully-restored 1960 Harley-Davidson FLH Duo Glide.**

for safety reasons. From 1974 until 1977, Harley-Davidson applied a rather crude solution to switch the shifting from the right to the left by simply running a secondary shaft underneath the frame, which was connected to an extremely long shift lever. It would be 1977 before Harley redesigned the transmission box to allow the gearshift shaft to exit to the left.

New models that were unveiled during these years included the first cruiser, the FX 1200 Super Glide (in 1971), the FXS Low Rider and the collectable XCLR (both 1977), as well as the FXEF Fat Bob (1979), while 1980 saw a flood of new arrivals in the FLT, FXB Sturgis, and FXWB Wide Glide. But, for the majority, the 1980s heralded the chance to turn around the fortunes of Harley-Davidson…

Up the Revolution!

With AMF running the company into the ground, consumer confidence at an all-time low, and the brand being nicknamed "Hardly-Ableson," June 1981 saw a rescue package put in place when 13 senior executives completed a management buyout of Harley-Davidson. The group was headed by Vaughn Beals (who would become chief executive) and Willie G. Davidson, the grandson of founder member William Davidson, who would serve as senior vice president and chief styling officer. It was Davidson who created the Super Glide and Low Rider that became so popular in the customization market.

The following year saw the introduction of the FXR/FXRS Super Glide and the adoption of a different stock system. Rather than tying up cash reserves, items were only ordered as and when necessary, lowering costs and having the added benefit of improving the build quality. The company petitioned the US International Trade Commission in response to the huge numbers of Japanese imports, and a tariff was imposed from April 1, 1983, on each imported machine over 43 ci (700 cc). This "tax" would run at decreasing rates for five years and allowed Harley-Davidson to build a loyal fan base by focusing on retro-styled motorcycles that harked back to the firm's glory days. The same year saw the foundation of the HOG, which has grown to include more than half a million members.

The 82 ci (1,340 cc) V2 Evolution engine, whose origins dated back seven years to the development begun during the AMF years, arrived in 1984. The new power unit proved reliable, required less frequent maintenance, and was, more importantly, oil-tight… something that could not be said about some of its predecessors. It was installed in several models, including the new Softail that featured a concealed rear suspension with a cantilever-swingarm design.

The boom years of the 1980s saw hardworking professionals with more disposable income available, and Harley-Davidson diversified into motorhomes for a decade with the acquisition of the

■ BELOW: **Harley-Davidson's senior vice president and chief styling officer, Willie G. Davidson, sits on a V-Rod outside the Willie G. Davidson Product Development Center in 2003.**

Holiday Rambler Corporation in December 1986. Recognizing that customers who had fallen in love with the brand were not getting any younger, perhaps the company strategists asked themselves why the discerning H-D enthusiast shouldn't have a recreational vehicle to relax in. By this time, the Harley-Davidson name was back in public ownership with a massive stock issue and the following year the company asked for the import tariff to end a year earlier than originally intended. The year of 1987 also saw the H-D stocks listed on the New York Stock Exchange and it seemed that the 84-year-old giant was back in the saddle and itching to compete with its Asian contemporaries. The company also launched a "Buy Back Program" that guaranteed a trade-in price when a customer upgraded from an XLH 883 Sportster to either an FL or FX.

The following year saw Harley-Davidson celebrating its 85th birthday with over 60,000 attending events in Milwaukee, the introduction of a Harley-Davidson Traveling Museum showcasing classic bikes and memorabilia, as well as the launch of two new motorcycles. Traditionalists welcomed the return of the sprung front end on the FXSTS Springer Softail while the Sportster 1200 arrived with a market-friendly $5,875 price tag. A use was found for 50 XR1000 engines that were surplus to H-D's requirements when they were supplied to Buell. It began an association with the sports bike company that would last for almost a quarter of a century.

The 1990s arrived with a flourish of new models and improvements: the FLSTF Fat Boy in 1990 and the Dyna family debuted the following year with the FXDB Dyna Glide Sturgis. In 1992, Harley-Davidson became the first manufacturer to fit the majority of their machines with drive belts that provided a smoother ride and offered less maintenance than chains. They also began work on a $31 million paint shop at the York, Pennsylvania plant that had been operational since 1973. In 1993, Harley-Davidson cemented their relationship with Buell by buying 49 per cent of the company stock (this would rise to 98 per cent in 1998 with H-D taking over complete ownership five years later) and the streets of Milwaukee rumbled with the noise of 100,000 celebrating the firm's 90th birthday

■ **ABOVE:** **A 1997 Harley-Davidson Low Rider is parked in front of the New York Stock Exchange in August 2005. Members of the Exchange were encouraged to ride their Harleys to work to celebrate the ringing of the closing bell by Harley-Davidson CEO Jim Ziemer.**

■ **BELOW:** **The Kings of the Highway, a group of Harley-Davidson owners, dominate a local highway in Japan during a once-a-month tour in 1992. Throughout the country there are more than a dozen Harley riding groups that have made Japan the largest foreign market for the US motorcycle maker.**

while fuel injection was introduced for the first time two years later with the 30th Anniversary Ultra Classic Electra Glide being the first recipient.

The second half of the 1990s saw a major expansion of the Harley-Davidson operation: the opening of a Parts and Accessories Distribution Center in Franklin, Wisconsin; a Product Development Center next to the Capitol Drive facility; new production plants in Menomonee Falls, Wisconsin, and Kansas City, Missouri; and an assembly center in Manaus, Brazil. By 1998, the number of Harley-Davidson enthusiasts celebrating the 95th anniversary had grown to more than 140,000 as the 20th century came to a successful conclusion. The number of motorcycles sold

throughout the 1990s had been phenomenal – especially when the company's inauspicious beginnings are taken into consideration – with around 170,000 machines produced in 1999 alone.

■ **ABOVE: The Arkansas State Harley Owners Group rally parade.**

■ **BELOW: Bruce Springsteen rides his 1994 Harley-Davidson Dyna Wide Glide on to the stage at the second annual Stand Up For Heroes in New York, 2008. The motorcycle was auctioned off with Springsteen's motorcycle jacket for $70,000.**

Into the 21st Century and Beyond

■ ABOVE: Inside the Harley-Davidson plant at the turn of the millennium.

The new millennium mirrored the end of the previous one, with the Softail family receiving a counter-balanced version of the twin cam 88 engine that had been installed in the Touring and Dyna models the year before. There were also two new motorcycles launched in the FXSTD Softail Deuce that boasted an 88 ci (1,440 cc) twin cam V-twin paired with a five-speed transmission, and the entry level 30 ci (492 cc) single cylinder OHV Buell Blast aimed at enticing new riders into the ever-growing Harley-Davidson family. To facilitate this, a beginner's course (Rider's Edge Academy of Motorcycling) was offered through Harley-Davidson and Buell dealerships. There was also a collaboration with Ford, who began production of the Ford F-150 Harley-Davidson Edition.

But the transition into the 21st

■ ABOVE: **Harley-Davidson introduces its new model for 2002 – the VRSCA V-Rod with its signature anodized aluminum body panels.**

century did not run smoothly on all fronts. There were claims of stock price manipulation in the late 1990s and early 2000s, while attempts by the company to trademark the distinctive engine sound of a Harley-Davidson only met with limited success and the US Patent Office application was not pursued. "I've personally spoken with Harley-Davidson owners from around the world," stated Joanne Bischmann (H-D's vice president of marketing) by means of an explanation as to why that particular avenue had been dropped, "and they've told me repeatedly that there is nothing like the sound of a Harley-Davidson motorcycle. If our customers know the sound cannot be imitated, that's good enough for me and for Harley-Davidson…"

Further innovations arrived with the launch of the VRSCA V-Rod, complete with fuel injection, liquid cooling, and overhead cams. With design input from Porsche, the 69 ci (1,130 cc) engine was capable of producing 115 hp and owed its heritage to the racing VR1000. The Buell Firebolt XB series made its arrival in 2002 with the XB9R but was beset by problems during its development that ran up costs and meant the market price was $2,000 more than the intended original of $7,995. As a result, despite its popularity as a quality motorcycle, it never sold in the quantities that Harley-Davidson anticipated.

One event that was greatly anticipated, however, was the Harley-Davidson centenary celebration. This kicked off with the start of the Open Road Tour in 2002 that culminated in the final event in Milwaukee the following year, attended by more than 250,000 people.

The Sportster models were revamped for 2004 (a new frame, rubber engine mounting, and a wider rear tire) and the FLHRSI Road King Custom was launched and boasted wide handlebars and a low rear ride height. A similar approach was added to the Sportster family the following year with the introduction of the XL 883 Low that placed the rider's seating position closer to the ground, while Harley-Davidson went for the retro look in the Softails. The FLSTN/I Softail Deluxe boasted a paint job that harked back to the 1939 range, and the FLSTSC/I Softail Springer Classic was a reminder of the classic motorcycles of the late 1940s.

The 2006 model range saw six-speed transmission included on the Dyna range (that welcomed the FXDB/I Street Bob) and a lowered Tourer in the FLHX/I Street Glide. It was also the year when the first H-D dealer was authorized in mainland China, thereby opening up another huge market to the company as the country's economic growth soared. The six-speed

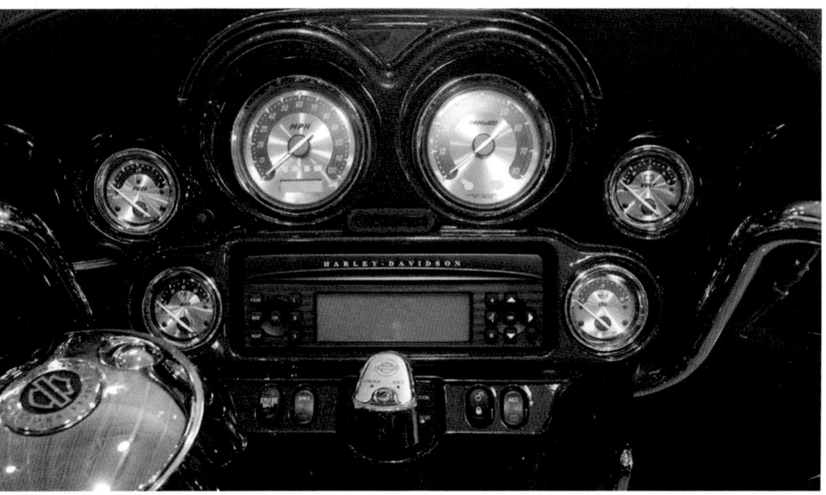

■ ABOVE: The Harley-Davidson 100th anniversary Traveling Museum, Los Angeles, 2002.

■ RIGHT: The console of Harley-Davidson's 2010 CVO Electra Glide Ultra Classic.

transmission was unilaterally rolled out the following year, the big twin engine was beefed up to a whopping 96 ci (1,573 cc), and 2007 also saw the launch of the first of the Dark Custom models in the XL1200N Nightster. It boasted unique features such as front fork gaiters, a bobbed rear fender, and a side-mounted LED-lit license plate.

The arrival of the FXCWC Rocker in 2008 heralded a swingarm-mounted rear fender and H-D's unusual Trick seat that looks like a solo saddle but can quickly be transformed into one that provides for a pillion passenger as well by unfolding its components. The Tourers received a new frame that lengthened the wheelbase, provided greater maneuverability, and a lowered seating position. The same year saw the opening of the Harley-Davidson Museum in Milwaukee and the company's acquisition of MV Agusta for $109 million. This was instigated to take advantage of MV's European distribution and paved the way for the introduction of the XR1200, a Sportster model specifically designed for the European market that proved so popular that it was eventually made available in the US as well.

Another global recession reared its unwelcome head toward the end of the 2000s and resulted in Harley-Davidson making difficult decisions as profits dropped 84 per cent in 2009 compared to the previous year. While the first three-wheeler aimed at the general public had been released with the 2009 launch of the FLHTCUTG Tri Glide Ultra Classic, the Buell line was discontinued and MV Agusta was sold-off in 2010. Harley-Davidson decided to target the growing market in India but the boom years of the late 20th century were over – two factories and a distribution center were closed and the company made the heartbreaking decision to axe a quarter of its workforce as massive restructuring took place in an effort to bring down overheads.

Not that this prevented the development and introduction of new models. The XL Forty-Eight (with its small gas tank styled in 1948 fashion) was added to the Sportster range in 2010, while the Softail Slim and Sportster Seventy-Two made their debuts in 2012.

It had been a long and exciting journey so far, but the Harley-Davidson brand could not rest on past glories… it had to adapt to the changing economic climate to stand any chance of being around to celebrate its bi-centennial.

■ BELOW: Harley-Davidson India's managing director, Anoop Prakash, presents a Harley-Davidson Fat Bob at its launch in New Delhi, India, 2012.

Model Families

Harley-Davidson models have long been grouped into "families" according to their designation and distinguishing features (like frame, engine, and suspension, etc.), although there is a certain amount of crossover that can lead to confusion. For example, the FLST is obviously an FL designated motorcycle but the FL part refers to the use of FL-type front forks on the Heritage Softail which is classed as a member of the softail family.

Since 1999, the Harley-Davidson Custom Vehicle Operations (CVO) team has designed limited edition customizations of stock models. Typically, two motorcycles are chosen to be modified each year and are the recipients of enhancements such as bigger engines, specialized paint jobs, performance upgrades, extra chrome or electronic accessories. While this is not an exhaustive list, meet the Harley-Davidson families and their main members.

■ ABOVE: H-D CEO Jim Ziemer poses on a 2008 Screamin' Eagle Dyna Custom cruiser in front of the New York Stock Exchange, 2007. Harley-Davidson celebrated its 20th anniversary of a listing on the NYSE.

Touring

Harley-Davidson touring motorcycles first made their appearance in 1941 with the launch of the FL and have been a favorite with enthusiasts ever since. Powered by a big V-twin engine, these behemoths of the highways are perfectly suited for the long, straight roads that crisscross the United States. Many clubs sprang up to enable likeminded people to explore the country, and comfort was high on their list of priorities.

Essential requirements included a comfortable riding position as well as equipment like panniers, a windshield, and headlights, and they were labeled "dressers," relating to the trend of loading the motorcycles with extras. As the decades passed by, full fairings equipped with radios and CBs became available and hard luggage containers replaced the original saddlebags.

The range is largely identified by its FL designation, although many have become known simply by their model names (such as the Electra Glide and Road Glide for instance). Members of the touring family are easily distinguishable by their fairings, the distinctive rear suspension, large-diameter telescopic front forks, and a luggage-carrying capability. The skeleton of the motorcycle remained largely unchanged from

■ **ABOVE: A Harley-Davidson FLHTK Electra Glide.**

Touring Models

Designation	*Model Name*
FLT	Tour Glide
FLH	Electra Glide
FLHS	Electra Glide Sport
FLHT	Electra Glide Standard
FLHTC	Electra Glide Classic
FLHTCU	Electra Glide Ultra Classic
FLHTK	Electra Glide Ultra Limited
FLHTCUTG	Tri Glide Ultra Classic
FLTR	Road Glide
FLTRX	Road Glide Custom
FLTRU	Road Glide Ultra
FLHR	Road King
FLHRC	Road King Classic
FLHRS	Road King Custom
FLTC	Tour Glide Classic
FLTCU	Tour Glide Ultra Classic
FLTRSEI	Screamin' Eagle Classic
FLHX	Street Glide

■ **ABOVE: The 1,450 cc Road King, in full police livery, as used by the Northumbria police force, England.**

1980 until 2009 when the range received a new frame, swingarm, and revised engine mountings.

The original FL was renamed the Hydra Glide in 1949 in honor of being the first Harley-Davidson to receive hydraulic telescopic front forks. Fast-forward nine years and the model name changed again, this time to the Duo Glide in recognition of the rear suspension with the swingarm utilizing a pair of coil sprung shock absorbers. The final redesignation of this series occurred in 1965 when the addition of electric starters saw the arrival of the Electra Glide.

Since then, further models (and their numerous variants) have been added to the family, with the Tour Glide, Road Glide, and Road King to name but a few. Harley-Davidson had long been a vehicle that was relatively easily customized and many trike conversions have been carried out over the years but there is now no longer such a pressing need, with the 2009 launch of the Tri Glide Ultra Classic. While the Servi-Car had been in production from 1932 until 1973, their use was mainly aimed at commercial enterprises and public service industries so this was the first trike for the general public.

■ **LEFT:** **Profile of a 2010 Harley-Davidson FLHXSE CVO Street Glide.**

Softail

The softail name is quite simply a description of the rear suspension. While early motorcycles had little or no ability to absorb any irregularities in the road, riders demanded more and more comfort. The softail design was first introduced by Harley-Davidson on the FXST Softail in 1984. Although the name was registered as a trademark, the term has gone on to be used to describe any motorcycle where the rear suspension components are hidden (much in the same way that vacuum cleaners are generally called Hoovers). In this way, the rider can enjoy a more comfortable experience while the motorcycle itself still resembles its hardtail ancestors of years gone by.

The technology to achieve this was developed in the mid-1970s by Bill Davis. An engineer by trade and a Harley-Davidson enthusiast by choice, Davis built a prototype using his 1972 Super Glide that boasted a cantilever swingarm that pivoted at the bottom but which was attached at the top by a spring/ shock absorber hidden underneath the seat. He patented this design but Willie G. Davidson was unconvinced. Undeterred, Davis set up his own firm to manufacture a revised design that set the pivot at the top with the springs/shocks under the frame. Marketed as the Road Worx Sub-Shock, the firm ran into difficulties and Davis ended up selling his idea and work so far to Harley-Davidson in January 1982, who further developed the system before the revolutionary design was unveiled in June 1983.

The majority of the many different Harley-Davidson Softail versions have been built around the same frame, engine, and transmission and only really differ in terms of fork, wheels, and accessories. The large-diameter FL-type forks are one option, as are the narrow X-type, depending on the width of the front wheel. The range has also been offered with the Springer forks that are reminiscent of the sprung forks used before the 1949 introduction of hydraulic telescopic ones.

■ OPPOSITE BELOW: A Harley-Davidson FLSTC Heritage Softail Classic.

■ BELOW: A Harley-Davidson Softail 88 ci engine.

Softail Models

Designation	*Model Name*
FXCW	Softail Rocker
FXCWC	Softail Rocker Custom
FXST	Softail Standard
FXSTC	Softail Custom
FXSTS	Springer Softail
FXSTD	Softail Deuce
FXS	Softail Blackline
FXSB	Softail Breakout
FXSTSB	Bad Boy
FLS	Softail Slim
FLST	Heritage Softail
FLSTF	Fat Boy
FLSTFB	Fat Boy Lo
FLSTC	Heritage Softail Classic
FLSTS	Heritage Springer Softail
FLSTSB	Cross Bones
FLSTSC	Softail Springer Classic
FLSTN	Heritage Softail Special – Nostalgia, Deluxe

Dyna

While the Dyna range is named after the chassis that was developed in the late 1980s and early 1990s, these motorcycles were traditionally labeled Super Glides and were introduced in 1971. Willie G. Davidson was aware of the passion that Harley-Davidson enthusiasts had for customizing their bikes and decided to create a motorcycle that could easily facilitate this. It gave the option of using the chassis of the larger H-D twin with components from the Sportster, like the front end.

Davidson had studied graphic art and worked for numerous automobile manufacturers before being headhunted to join the Harley-Davidson design department in 1963. He had experienced the thriving custom scene for himself in California and had been designing motorcycles as a sideline. Davidson's initial offerings were not always well received by the H-D management who were more set in their ways. They believed the company should continue offering traditional motorcycles, but sense won out in the end and a whole new customer base was acquired.

For his first machine in the family, Davidson added the telescopic forks from the Sportster to the frame and rear suspension of the Electra Glide and it was designated the FX (Factory Experimental) Super Glide. With the addition of buckhorn handlebars (often nicknamed "mini-apes," they are a variation on the ape hanger that forces the rider to reach up), the new machine began to take on a chopper-style look, but the adoption of a Sportster-like rear fender unit wasn't universally popular. Once the "boattail" rear end was modified, sales figures improved and this was replicated in the Sportster.

The Super Glide is seen by many as a landmark motorcycle that boosted the company image as well as its sales figures. It has since undergone many variants and become one of Harley-Davidson's best-selling ranges. There was also a "convertible" option – which might sound strange to some – but the description meant that the rider could remove the windshield as and when desired.

■ **BELOW LEFT: A Harley-Davidson FXDWG Dyna Wide Glide.**

■ **BELOW: A 1991 Harley-Davidson Dyna Glide Sturgis on the way down from Lolo Pass on US 12 in Idaho.**

Dyna Models

Designation	*Model Name*
FXD	Dyna Super Glide
FXDB	Dyna – Street Bob
FXDB-D	Dyna Glide Daytona – Belt
FXDB-S	Dyna Glide Sturgis – Belt
FXDC	Dyna Super Glide Custom
FXDF	Dyna – Fat Bob
FXDG	Dyna Glide Sturgis
FXDX	Dyna Glide Super Sport
FXDS-CONV	Dyna Glide Convertible
FXDXT	Dyna Super Glide T Sport
FXDL	Dyna Low Rider
FXDWG	Dyna Wide Glide
FLD	Dyna Switchback

Sportster

Light, fast, and highly desirable, the Sportster (designation XL) was launched in 1957 as a replacement for the K flathead motorcycle and is now considered by most experts to be America's first muscle bike. With a 55 ci (900 cc) OHV engine, the 1957 Sportster was created in response to the imported British sports bikes of the time, but few could have predicted that it would become the longest-running motorcycle model in history, with production continuing well into the 21st century. The Harley-Davidson Sportster is still going strong more than 50 years after its arrival and is still based very much on the original 1957 design, although now comes in 54 ci (883 cc) and 73 ci (1,200 cc) options.

In 1952, the Model K Sport and Sport Solo motorcycles were introduced but are not always considered by everyone to be

Sportster Models

Designation	*Model Name*
XL	4-Speed 883 Sportster
XL883	883 Hugger
XL883C	883 Custom
XL883L	SuperLow
XL883N	Iron 883
XL1100	Standard 1100
XL1200	Standard 1200
XL1200C	1200 Custom
XL1200L	1200 Low
XL1200N	1200 Nightster
XL1200R	1200 Roadster
XL1200S	1200 Sport
XL1200X	Forty-Eight
XL1200V	Seventy-Two
XLCH	4-Speed 883 Kick Start
XLCR	Café Racer 1000
XLH	4-Speed 883 Electric Start
XLH883	883 Hugger
XLH1200	Standard 1200
XLH1200S	Sport
XLS	4-Speed Roadster
XLX	4-Speed 1000
XR1000	1000 with Competition Heads

■ BELOW: **Static profile view of an orange 2008 Harley-Davidson 105th Anniversary Sportster Custom motorcycle.**

Sportsters, although they are definitely the inspiration for the development of the Sportster family. The first Sportster featured many of the same details of the KH including the frame, fenders, large gas tank, and front suspension, and boasted a right-hand shift, full suspension, and a four-speed transmission.

The company didn't use their dealerships to introduce their latest motorcycle, instead they premiered it at regional gatherings, but the Sportster became nationally famous in the United States in 1968 with a headlining role in the hit TV series *Then Came Bronson*, starring Michael Parks. Partly because of this, but more so because the Sportster is the least expensive Harley-Davidson and is more suitable for those of a smaller stature, it has been very popular with entry-level riders, and women. It has been produced in numerous variants, some of which – like the Café Racer and the XR1000 – are beginning to appreciate in value as they become more and more collectible.

■ ABOVE: Daredevil cyclist Evel Knievel as he warms up on his Harley-Davidson outside Madison Square Garden on Seventh Avenue in New York City.

VRSCs (V-Rods)

The introduction of the VRSC (V-twin Racing Street Custom) in 2001 left many purists wondering which direction Harley-Davidson was taking in their design of motorcycles. It was totally different from anything the company had ever produced before but it was another masterstroke by Willie G. Davidson, while the marketing statement read, "It's time to challenge the senses and the status quo."

Developed to compete with other muscle bikes on the power cruiser market, the V-Rod oozes sex appeal and comes equipped with the Revolution engine. This power plant was designed with the help of German giants Porsche and features overhead cams as well as liquid cooling. The motorcycle is distinctive because of its 60-degree angled V-twin engine and its unusual placement of the gas tank, which is sited under the seat, although the streamlining on top of the frame is reminiscent of its traditional position but is purely "window dressing."

The V-Rod divided opinions like no other Harley-Davidson before. Jim McGraw (*New York Times*) claimed "Many riders don't know what to make of the new V-Rod from Harley-Davidson," while another reviewer described the riding experience as "… deft maneuvering and aggressive engineering. Make no mistake, the V-Rod lets you know it still has the heart and soul of a Harley when you crack that throttle, so hold fast and ride hard."

But the introduction of the V-Rod was a necessity in a time of legislation to control emissions and noise pollution without compromising the Harley-Davidson heritage. Aluminum components and body panels made the overall weight of the machine lighter, while the latest aerodynamic styling improved performance. Some thought that the overall look of the V-Rod differed too much from the H-D tradition but were reassured by the angle of the raked forks and the positioning of the forward controls that at least bore some

VRSC (V-Rod) Models

Designation	***Model Name***
VRSCA	V-Rod with more options
VRSCB	Basic V-Rod
VRSCAW	V-Rod
VRSCR	Street Rod
VRSCD	Night Rod
VRSCDX	Night Rod Special
VRSCF	V-Rod Muscle

■ RIGHT: A Harley-Davidson Night Rod Special with modified exhaust.

■ BELOW: The VRSCA V-Rod in full motion.

familial resemblance. Early versions produced complaints that the riding position was not comfortable, so amendments were made to the Anniversary and Night Rod Special editions, versions of the VRSCDX that did not stretch the rider as far.

Whatever your opinion on the VRSC, the range has proved its longevity and has been made more than welcome in the Harley-Davidson family circle…

Military Service

It seems only natural that a great American icon would be the perfect partner for the United States military in hazardous situations all around the globe, but that association dates back to the Mexican Expedition (also known as the Pancho Villa Expedition) that took place between March 1916 and February 1917. The operation saw the 5,000 men of the US Army – led by General "Black Jack" Pershing – pursuing Francisco "Pancho" Villa in retaliation for the Mexican revolutionary leader's attack on the town of Columbus, New Mexico. The objective was simple: put a stop to his paramilitary activities and facilitate his capture… dead or alive. Pershing believed in using the latest technology available to him so employed aircraft and trucks for the first time. He also used Harley-Davidsons with machine guns mounted in sidecars in pursuit of the Mexicans, but was ultimately unsuccessful with Villa being wounded but escaping and surviving until he was assassinated in July 1923. The motorcycle, however, had proved a useful asset and the War Department put in an order for a dozen Harley-Davidsons that was later doubled.

The First World War saw civilian models being adapted for military use before the development of the FUS and LUS. These machines were more suited to battlefield conditions and included flat fenders that were positioned higher than they would normally be to cater for the uneven, often muddy terrain. They had also proved their worth as couriers in an era before reliable radio communication. By the end of the conflict, around 20,000 Harley-

LEFT: General "Black Jack" Pershing, at the head of his men, fords a stream in Mexico in 1916 while leading the United States troops there in pursuit of "Pancho" Villa.

BELOW: The Harley-Davidson Motor Co. built more than 90,000 motorcycles for the armed forces during the Second World War. A row of Army Armored Division mounted soldiers made an impressive sight.

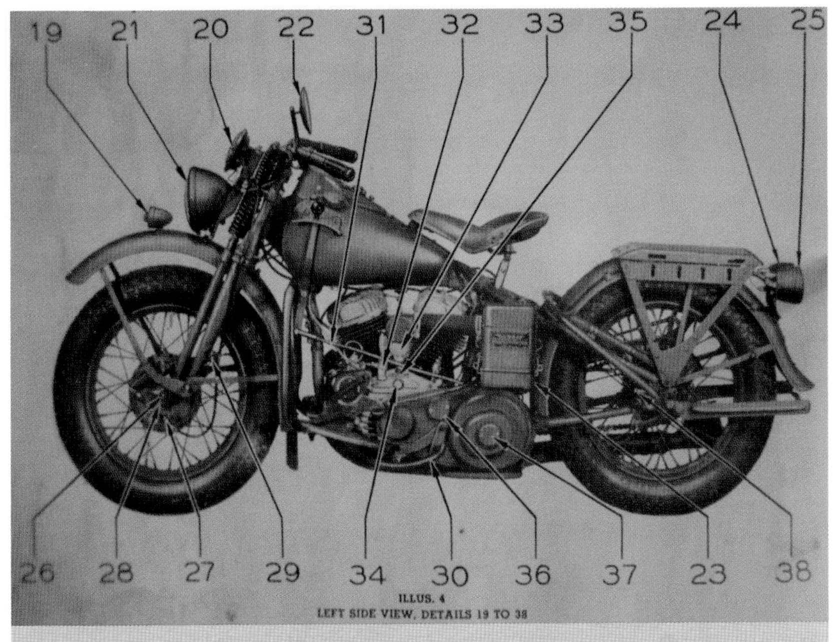

■ ABOVE: The left side of a Harley-Davidson WLA, with detail annotations, from the US War Department Operation and Maintenance Manual TM-10-1175, published in 1942.

Davidsons had taken part in the war effort but co-ordination between H-D and the military did not cease with a return to civilian life. There was talk of a three-wheeled vehicle being developed during the 1930s, but this ultimately did not see the light of day.

The Second World War saw Harley-Davidson being asked – along with their main competitor, Indian – to come up with a motorcycle that was perfectly suited to military desert warfare requirements. H-D's answer was the XA 750 but it never saw combat because the conflict zones had changed by the time it was ready for action and the Jeep was already proving a more versatile vehicle. The WLA (with the WLC being the Canadian Army version) was, however, prevalent and more than 70,000 were sent into action by the time the hostilities ended in May 1945. Harley-Davidson was presented with several Army-Navy "E" Awards for Excellence in Wartime Production for their consistently high-quality motorcycles.

The WLA was again produced between 1949 and 1952, while military Sportsters were manufactured in small numbers in the 1960s. These motorcycles saw action in far-flung parts of the world, including Indonesia and Vietnam. The last motorcycles produced for the military were the MT-500 and MT-350E during the 1990s following Harley-Davidson's acquisition of Armstrong-CCM Motorcycles in 1987. The MT-500 was already in production and had been on active service with the British Army in the Falklands War of 1982 but later supply was restricted to Canada and Jordan. Production of the MT ceased in 1998 as Harley-Davidson was finally demobbed from the army.

Equipping the Police

■ ABOVE: **A close-up of a police issue Harley-Davidson motorcycle's 96-CID twin cam engine used by the Berkley Police Department, 2008.**

■ OPPOSITE: **The Philadelphia Police Department's Harley-Davidson motorcycles.**

Harley-Davidson's association with law enforcement agencies is now more than a century old. The first motorcycle sold for police duty was delivered to the Detroit, Michigan Police Department as far back as 1908, when the company was only five years old. It hadn't taken Harley-Davidson long at all to build up a reputation for reliability and this, combined with its versatility over uneven ground and unmade roads, made it the perfect vehicle for protecting rural areas. The first official motorcycle police patrol was organized in 1911 by Chief August Vollmer of the Berkley, California Police Department. Of course, with the introduction of prohibition – the national ban on the production, transportation, and sale of alcohol in the United States between 1920 and 1933 – motorcycles were the perfect way of enforcing this law.

The number of H-Ds on police duty rose rapidly during the 1920s, as numerous states set up their own police forces. At the start of the decade, six men on Harley-Davidsons made up the Washington State Troopers, while 16 patrolmen had to cover the whole state of Louisiana. It was also a time when all forms of vehicles were being developed and improved, leading to busier roads, higher speeds, and rising numbers of fatalities on the highways. The motorcycle was ideally suited for getting to the scene of an accident quickly or chasing an offender to enforce the law. A dedicated office was set up for fleet sales to numerous law enforcement agencies that had rocketed to more than 3,000 by the end of the 1920s.

Harley-Davidson suffered during the Great Depression but managed to survive with marketing focusing on the benefits of its motorcycle to the police. The Servi-Car was introduced in 1931, and was an instant hit with law enforcement agencies across the nation, with the three-wheeler becoming a regular sight over the next five decades.

It seemed that each decade brought with it different issues for the police to deal with. The 1950s saw street racing rise in popularity, with teenagers souping-up jalopies to create hot rods. These competitions culminated in the formation of a Hot Rod Squad by

■ BELOW: **Philadelphia police officers park their Harley-Davidson motorcycles, 2010.**

Harley-Davidson patrol officers of the Pittsburgh Police Department. The 1960s brought civil unrest, student radicalism, and protests against the war in Vietnam, while the latter part of the 20th century saw a rise in gangs and drug-related crime.

After the terrorist attacks of September 11, 2001, the company donated 37 motorcycles to the New York Police Department, the Port Authority of New York and New Jersey, and the New York State Police. The sale of Harley-Davidsons to police departments

■ ABOVE: **Former Vice President Dan Quayle sits on one of the Harley-Davidsons used by the Nassau County Police who escorted him during his visit to Long Island in Farmingdale, New York, 1992.**

more than doubled during the first decade of the 21st century. In the United States, more than 3,400 police departments are equipped with H-Ds – in contrast to the 400 of 20 years earlier – while they are also found in 45 countries around the world.

Harley-Davidson's role in law enforcement is not restricted to the supply of motorcycles though. The company has a long association with the Northwestern University Center for Public Safety (formerly the Traffic Institute) and does much to promote officer training and public safety awareness.

It's a fairly safe bet that wherever you are, there's a cop on a Harley-Davidson ready to protect you…

■ ABOVE: Harley-Davidson police motorcycles donated by the Bureau of International Narcotics and Law Enforcement Affairs to the Lebanese Internal Security Forces, at the US Embassy, Beirut, 2010.

A Racing Pedigree

As previously mentioned, Bill Harley headed up the newly created Harley-Davidson Racing Department in 1912, and it wasn't long before the trophy cabinet began bulging at the seams. Walter Davidson had already proved the motorcycle's capability, with a perfect score in the 1908 FAM Endurance and Reliability Contest that saw 65 riders tackle a 365-mile course in New York's Catskill Mountains over a two-day event. The intervention of the First World War saw racing suspended but the factory racing team earned the nickname the "Wrecking Crew" as a result of their domination, while their pig mascot gave Harley-Davidson its "hog" moniker.

Otto Walker was captain of the H-D team in 1921, and set the record books alight in Fresno, California, on February 22, when he became the first racer to average more than 100 mph (160 kmh) en route to winning a motorcycle race. He also earned the distinction of winning the most races at any one meet that day. Not to be outdone, English racer Douglas Davidson (no relation) registered the first official 100 mph over a timed course in Britain three months later. It seemed that no one could compete with the Harley-Davidsons and three years later H-D riders claimed all eight races in the National Championships.

The company signed Joe Petrali as a salaried factory racer in 1925, and he went on to become one of the best racers of all time during the 1930s. Bill Jackson (manager of the Harley-Davidson Archives) said, "Every sport has had its legendary heroes… the sport of motorcycle racing had its own hero, Joe

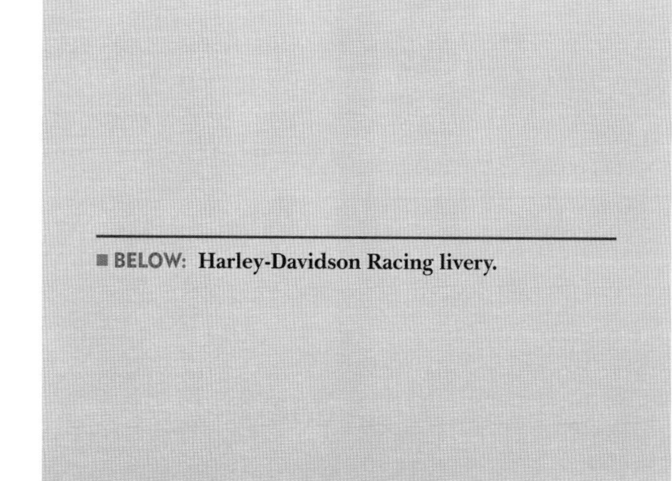

■ BELOW: Harley-Davidson Racing livery.

Petrali, a star whose championship performances have never been matched and not even approached." Petrali went on to establish his own legend on two wheels with five consecutive national dirt track championships and eight hill-climb titles, as well as a new land speed record of 136.183 mph (219.165 kmh) in 1937 on a modified 61 ci (1,000 cc) V-twin Streamliner, at Daytona Beach.

Daytona has been a happy hunting ground for Harley-Davidson and their riders, with three crowns being won by Ben Campanale and Babe Tancrede on WLDR models between 1938 and 1940. By the time competition resumed after the Second World War, Petrali had retired but the introduction of the 45 ci (737 cc)

■ **ABOVE: A Harley-Davidson 1914 racing motorcycle.**

WR kept the Harley-Davidson name at the top of the rostrum and it went on to earn legendary status as a racing machine.

The American Motorcyclist Association (AMA) had created a Class C competition during the 1930s to reduce the costs for entrants. This new class allowed for limited modifications to street-legal production motorcycles so that racing was less expensive and more accessible to the average motorcyclist than the Class A prototype-based racing. The AMA inaugurated its Grand National Championship in 1954 that was initially dominated by Harley-Davidson riders with Joe Leonard (1954 and 1956-57), Brad Andres (1955), Carroll Resweber (1958-1961), and Bart Markel (1962) all

■ **LEFT:** Carroll Resweber, one of the H-R riders who dominated the Grand National Championship.

■ **BELOW:** Lance Weil from California – one of the first Americans to race in Europe – riding an 833 cc Harley-Davidson at Brands Hatch, England, 1967.

being crowned champion before Dick Mann's BSA provided a slight blip in continuity in 1963. Whereas the Grand National champions from 1946 until 1953 had been crowned on the basis of a single race, the revised format saw five different competitions (four being held on dirt tracks with the fifth on asphalt). It would take the arrival of Gary Nixon on a Triumph in 1967 to break the domination of the Harley-Davidsons.

By 1953, however, the WR and WRTT were being outclassed by the invading British 500s, so the 750 cc flathead KR was developed in the early 1950s. The 1950s and 1960s saw H-D riders win the trophy on 13 occasions on KR and KRTT models, with Brad Andres crossing the finishing line in first place three times, although Cal Rayborn's 1969 victory proved to be the company's last of the 20th century as its economic woes put an end to the road racing team. Rayborn wrote his name in the record books the following year when his Streamliner set a new motorcycle world land speed record of 254.84 mph (405.25 kmh) on the Bonneville salt flats near Wendover, Utah.

The dirt track team's success continued, however, with Jay Springsteen registering three consecutive titles between 1976 and 1978. By this time, the XR 750 had been introduced under revised AMA rules for Class C racing. The new motorcycle – based on the Sportster – was more powerful, extremely reliable, and succeeded in dominating the sport.

Harley-Davidson signed Scott Parker to the team in 1981, and he went on to become the most successful competitor in the

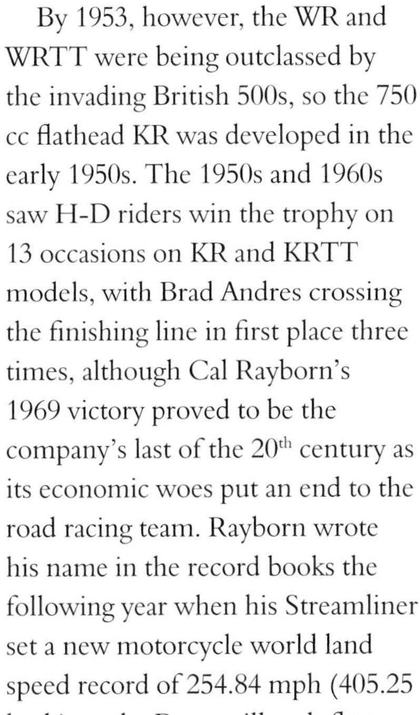

■ BELOW INSET: **A 1980 Harley-Davidson XR 750.**

company's history, racking up more than 90 career victories and claiming nine Grand National Championships by the end of the 1990s.

The team returned to road racing in 1994, when the VR1000 was entered into the AMA Superbike Championship. Despite promising performances, however, this model would never win a race before it retired in 2001, but it did provide the platform for the development of electronic fuel injection and liquid cooling that would make the transition into production bikes.

Road racing's loss though was drag racing's gain, as the Screamin'

■ BELOW: **Andrew Hines on his Screamin' Eagle/ Vance & Hines Pro Stock motorcycle leaves the line for his first qualifying run at Pontiac Excitement Nationals at the National Trail Raceway in Kirkersville. Hines set a new track record on his way to being the top qualifier in the Pro Stock Bike Division, 2004.**

Eagle/Vance & Hines Pro Stock Motorcycle team was launched in 2002. Two years later, Andrew Hines staked his claim as the youngest champion in NHRA history when he claimed the NHRA POWERade Pro Stock Motorcycle Championship at the age of 21. By 2006, he had won three consecutive titles before team-mate Eddie Krawiec got in on the action.

It was a similar story on the dirt flat tracks as well, with Kenny Coolbeth dominating the opposition on his XR 750 and Danny Eslick winning the inaugural AMA Pro Vance & Hines XR1200 Series Championship. It seemed that history was repeating itself. Just as Harley-Davidsons had dominated the beginning of the 20th century, so they seemed to be the motorcycles to beat as the 21st century got under way…

■ LEFT: **Kenny Coolbeth: 2006 flat track national champion.**

Customizing your Harley-Davidson

The trend of customizing Harley-Davidsons has been around for many, many years, with blood, sweat, and tears often being an integral part of the process – but that doesn't have to be the norm in the 21st century. Today, the CVO team builds special edition motorcycles based around current stock models, while the Harley-Davidson website offers the chance to tailor your own machine to your personal needs in terms of fit, function, style, and performance. But this wasn't always the case and H-D riders have long had a habit of wanting to stand out among the crowd.

In the mid-20th century, choices were limited, with two distinct families of V-twin Harley-Davidsons – the small twin or the big twin (providing you disregard the Servi-Car) – available between 1934 and 1970. It didn't take a mechanical genius, however, to do some basic customization by changing parts between bikes or – for the more ambitious – cutting and welding frames and other components to bring their creations to life.

In truth, Harley-Davidsons were slower than their British counterparts (although more reliable) and tuning was an expensive way of enhancing performance. A simpler route was to discard some unnecessary equipment, such as front fenders, windshields, and saddlebags. Even the rear fender was chopped and gave rise to a particular style of bike in the California Bobber. The

chopper made it onto the scene in the 1950s with the arrival of extended forks. No one seems to be sure why this adaptation occurred but it was soon realized that it was a relatively easy job to weld an extra piece on to extend the forks by the desired length. The technological advance that came with hydraulic telescopic forks was not universally adopted, as the Harley-Davidson springer was still one of the most adaptable and suited the stripped-down style. After extending the forks, it was a natural progression to give the handlebars the same treatment and they grew into buckhorns, high risers, and finally ape hangers with the pillion sissy bar being stretched as well.

As it turned out, the obsession with customizing motorcycles led to the creation of a new industry, with more and more firms offering components, accessories, and custom paint jobs. This grew to such an extent in the 1970s that Harley-Davidson realized the error of its ways and began catering for the customization market themselves with the introduction of the Super Glide. Since then, many new models have been introduced that provide for those who like to be a bit different…

The Harley-Davidson Culture

■ **ABOVE: The annual Sturgis Motorcycle Rally gathering of motorcycle enthusiasts.**

Maybe it's the feeling of being alone on the open road or the pleasure of being able to weave through traffic jams but motorcyclists have long felt an affinity with one another that is not replicated by those driving automobiles. The early riders formed clubs or associations that allowed groups of like-minded individuals to enjoy their pursuit with others and began to organize events. The first Black Hills Rally (now the Sturgis Motorcycle Rally) in Sturgis, South Dakota, was held on August 14, 1938, by the Jackpine Gypsies motorcycle club.

In 1947, Harley-Davidson began sales of an item of clothing that would forever be associated with bikers in the black leather motorcycle jacket that was adopted as a "uniform" by many servicemen returning to the United States after serving their country in the Second World War. Disheartened by their experiences and disillusioned upon their return to find the best jobs already taken, many struggled to adjust to civilian life and rebelled against the discipline they had been subject to. They splashed out on a motorcycle and formed their own groups of comrades with names that epitomized their attitudes, such as Pissed Off Bastards and Satan's Sinners preceding the Hell's Angels. Isolated incidents of public disorder and violence soon led to an increase in the number of disaffected youngsters swelling their ranks and a tarnished reputation that motorcyclists of the 21st century are still struggling to shrug off.

Stanley Kubrick's *The Wild One* addressed the issue in 1953, with Marlon Brando and Lee Marvin playing the leaders of two rival motorcycle gangs, while *Easy Rider* (1969) was another movie that focused on two diverse bikers in Peter Fonda and Dennis Hopper. The silver screen was a powerful

■ **ABOVE: Peter Fonda and Dennis Hopper in *Easy Rider*.**

marketing tool that was exploited to the extreme, but print was another avenue. Harley-Davidson was keen to market their machines to potential customers from all walks of life, and the image of a young Elvis Presley, sat astride a KH model on the cover of the May 1956 issue of *Enthusiast*, wouldn't have harmed sales at all…

The advertising obviously worked because white-collar workers and qualified professionals were not put off owning a Harley-Davidson. By 1997, one report stated that the average household income for H-D riders was around $83,000 – a figure that had more than doubled in the previous decade. The average age of the typical Harley-Davidson rider was also on the increase, perhaps because those who had been loyal to the brand were ageing themselves and/or due to the fact that people suffering a mid-life crisis often tended to try to relive their youth.

The Harley-Davidson Owners Group was established in 1983 to cater for the burgeoning fascination with their motorcycles, and five years later the company's Traveling Museum hit the road to coincide with the 85th birthday celebration. It offered visitors the chance to see classic motorcycles, memorabilia, and explore the company's rich history. A similar display went on the road to commemorate the Harley-Davidson centenary during 2002-03 that focused both on the company's heritage and its future.

A more permanent exhibition opened in 2008 with the Harley-Davidson Museum in Milwaukee, a three-building complex that boasts more than 450 motorcycles and attracts around 300,000 visitors every year.